Earth, Water, Fire, Air

A Suite for Voices, Narrator and Orff Instruments

Don Dupont

and

Brian Hiller

ISBN 0-934017-60-3

Michael D. Bennett, editor
Richard Knowles, cover artist

Memphis Musicraft Publications
Box 981, Rociada, NM 87742

Dedication

To my parents, Cynthia and Donald E. DuPont, for their love, support and guidance.
Don Dupont

In loving memory of my father, Charles Hiller.
Brian Hiller

Cover Art

front: *World III*, watercolor, 2005, by Richard Knowles
back: *World IV*, watercolor, 2005, by Richard Knowles

© 2005, Memphis Musicraft Publications

All rights reserved. No part of this publication
may be reproduced or distributed in any form
without the expressed permission of the
publisher. Exception: The Melody Appendix
may be copied for single classroom student use.

Contents

Preface iv

Prologue 1
    Round and Round 1

Earth 2
    Earth 2
    La Tierra 3

Water 5
    Earth, Water 5
    Wade in the Water 6

Fire 8
    Earth, Water, Fire 8
    Tina Singu 9

Air 11
    Earth, Water, Fire, Air 11
    Riding on the Wind 12
    Round and Round (reprise) 14

Melody Appendix 15

Fine Arts Connections 19

Preface

Earth, Water, Fire, Air: A Suite for Voices, Narrator and Orff Instruments is a performance piece celebrating the natural "elements" of Earth, Water, Fire and Air. The songs feature unison, two and three-part singing, speech ostinati, instrumental accompaniments, recorder playing and movement suggestions.

The songs in the suite can be used in several ways:

* As a suite they weave together with the poems and connecting music to form an exciting performance piece for upper-grade ensembles.
* Each song can stand alone and be used to teach specific skills and concepts or demonstrate different musical forms at any point in your curriculum.
* The suite or songs may form the core for a school-wide Earth Day celebration. Younger students can sing the songs accompanied by older students. Your art, physical education, librarian and classroom teachers can all help integrate artwork, movement, literature and poetry into an exciting presentation.

We have written cinquain poems to preface each section of the suite. Cinquains are 22 syllable, five line poems with the following structure: 1st line-two syllables, 2nd line-four syllables, 3rd line-six syllables, 4th line-eight syllables, 5th line-two syllables. The poems can be enhanced using sound color and movement if desired. They can be spoken chorally, in small groups or by single narrators, which is the method shown in the text. Students may also wish to write their own cinquains after becoming familiar with the form.

In the *Song Appendix* we have included the vocal parts for each song with chord symbols for use with piano or guitar if you do not have an Orff Instrumentarium. Also included in *Fine Arts Connections* are several art and music suggestions which can extend the suite's overall experience for your students. These examples can be found in most school libraries and by searching on the internet.

The beauty of Orff-Schulwerk is allowing your students to create, explore and improvise using their ideas. We encourage you to adapt this suite to the needs and abilities of your students.

We wish to acknowledge Lynn Palmer for her valuable insight into the *Fine Arts Connections* and Don Bennett, our editor, for his belief in and dedication to this project.

Don Dupont
Brian Hiller

Prologue

Narrator:
Ancient peoples believed that Earth, Water, Fire and Air were the essential building blocks of the world. Like the seasons, which allowed them to live in harmony with the universe, these "elements" helped create a balance. Although each "element" had its own distinct personality, they were woven together in art, dance and music to create a perfect balance to sustain life.

Round and Round
   Intro: BM tremolo, four measures.

Round and Round

Traditional
Arr. Dupont/Hiller

Rubato

Round and round the world is turn-ing. Turn-ing al-ways 'round to morn-ing. And from morn-ing 'round to night.

♩ = 130

Earth, wat - er, fire and air.

Canon

① Round and round the world is turn-ing. Turn-ing al-ways
   Earth, wat-ter, fire and air. Earth, wat-er,

② ③ 'round to morn-ing. And from morn-ing 'round to night.
   fire and air. Earth, wat - er, fire and air.

-1-

Earth

Narrator: Stability, Wisdom, Strength, Growth!

All: Earth! (followed by a cluster chord on all barred instruments in C Pentatonic).

Narrator:
Noble
In its virtue;
All we are, all we know;
Sacred ground nurtures and yields such
Beauty.

Earth (From *Earth, Water, Fire, Air*. See page 11.)
   Form: Additive
      (1) accompaniment, (2) V4.

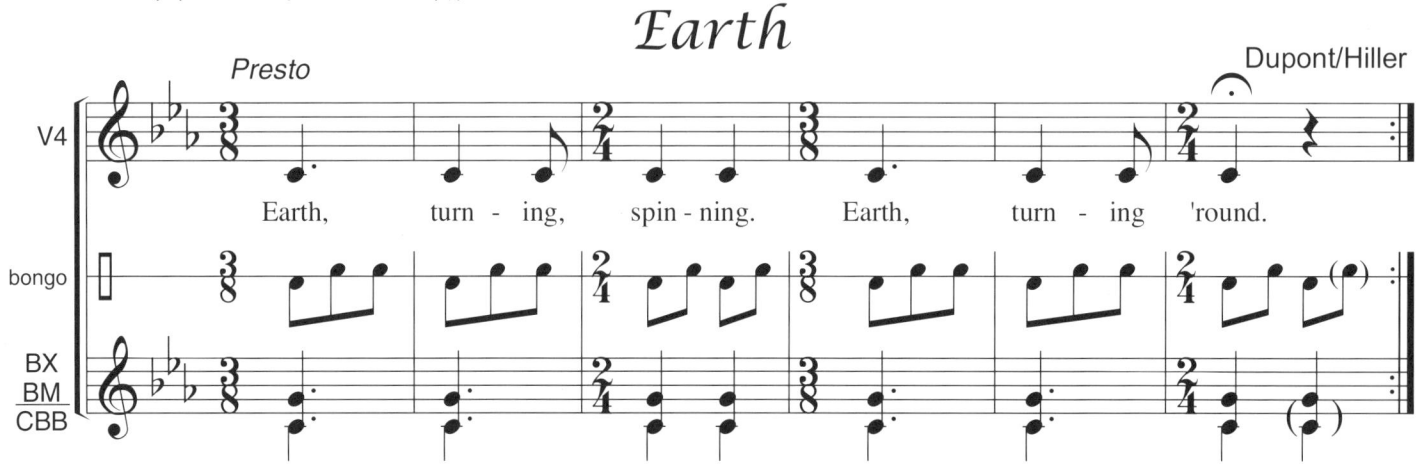

Earth

Presto — Dupont/Hiller

Earth, turn-ing, spin-ning. Earth, turn-ing 'round.

La Tierra
   Form: Intro: first four measures of accompaniment.
      Verse 1 / Chorus
      Verse 2 / Chorus

   Movement: Circles of 8. Hands held in W position.

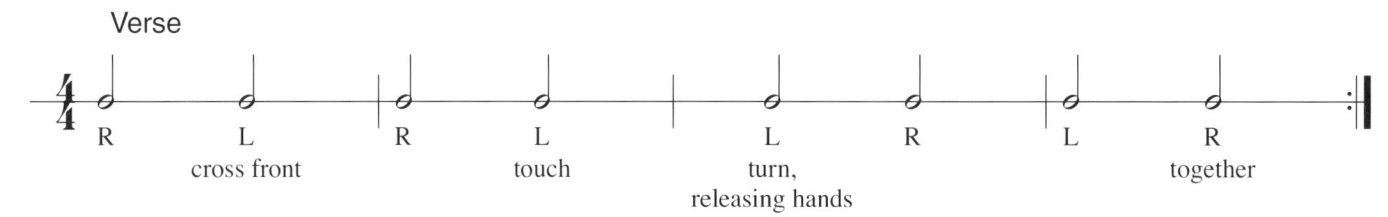

Verse
R L R L L R L R
   cross front   touch   turn,   together
               releasing hands

Chorus: Individual movement improvisation.

Translation:
Sing to the Earth,
Sing loud and clear,
Dance to the Earth,
Dance with your soul.

La Tierra

Verse ♩ = 112

Dupont/Hiller

1. We sing for Earth and for beau-ty. We dance for all she pro-vides. We lift our hearts and our voi-ces, and cel-e-brate side by side.
2. Oh, Moth-er Earth, we re-spect you. Your moun-tains, val-leys and shores. We stand as one to pro-tect you, and care for you ev-er-more.

Chorus

Cante a la Tierra. Cante fuerte y claro.

Chorus 1, no repeats.
Chorus 2, three times with final ending.

Baile a la Tierra. Baile con su al - ma. ma.

Water

Narrator: Emotion, Love, Mystery, Compassion!

All: Water! (followed by a cluster chord on all barred instruments in C Pentatonic).

Narrator:
Flowing
Raindrops gather;
Stream, river, ocean, sea;
Mighty, rhythmic waves of freedom
Resound!

Earth, Water
Form: Additive
(1) accompaniment, (2) V4, (3) V3.

Earth, Water

Dupont/Hiller

Presto

V3: Wa - ter slow - ly ris - ing. Wa - ter slow - ly ris - ing.

V4: Earth, turn - ing, spin - ning. Earth, turn - ing 'round.

bongo

BX
BM
CBB

Wade in the Water
Form: Additive, then subtractive! Each segment is 12 measures in length.
- A   Conga alone (4 bars), then add V1 (8 bars).
- AB   Conga and bongos (4 bars), then add V1 and V2 (8 bars).
- ABC   Conga, bongos, and maracas (4 bars), then add V1, V2, and V3 (8 bars).
- BC   Remove V1 (all percussion continue).
- B   Remove V3 (all percussion continue).
- Coda   Remove V2 (all percussion gradually fade out).

Movement: Three concentric circles (V1 - outer, V2 - inner, V3 - middle). Each group moves only when singing its part.

Wade in the Water

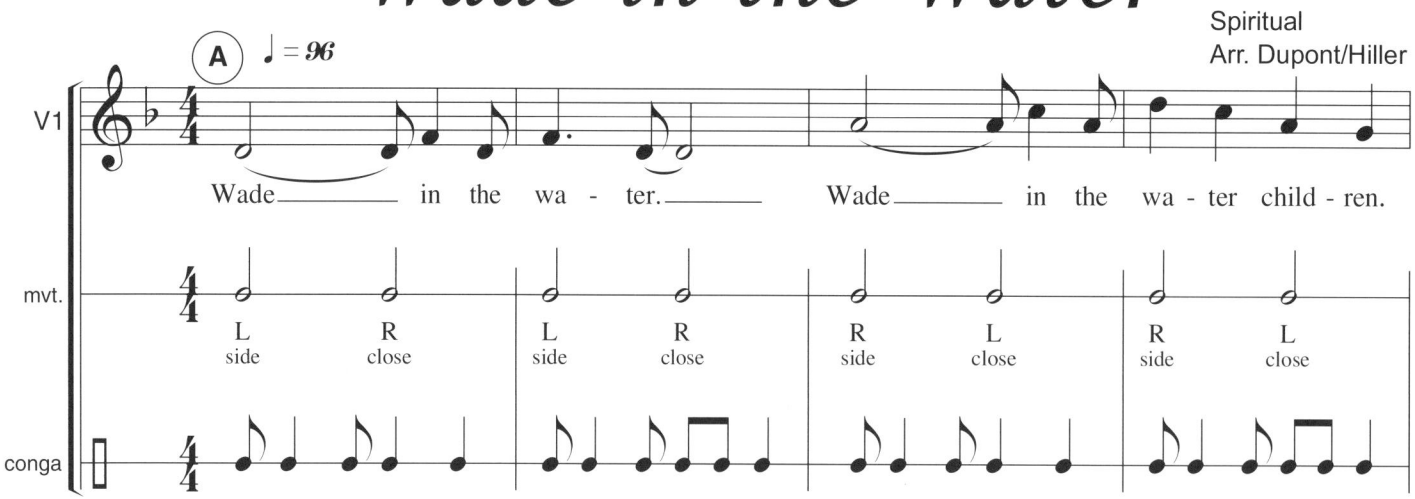

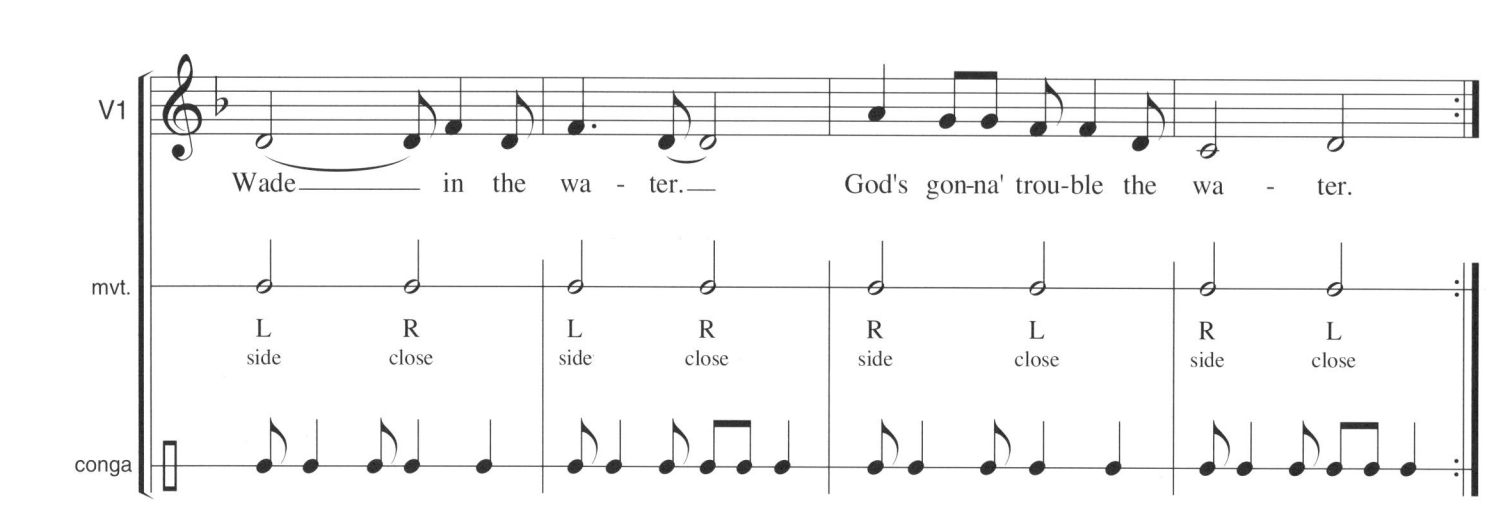

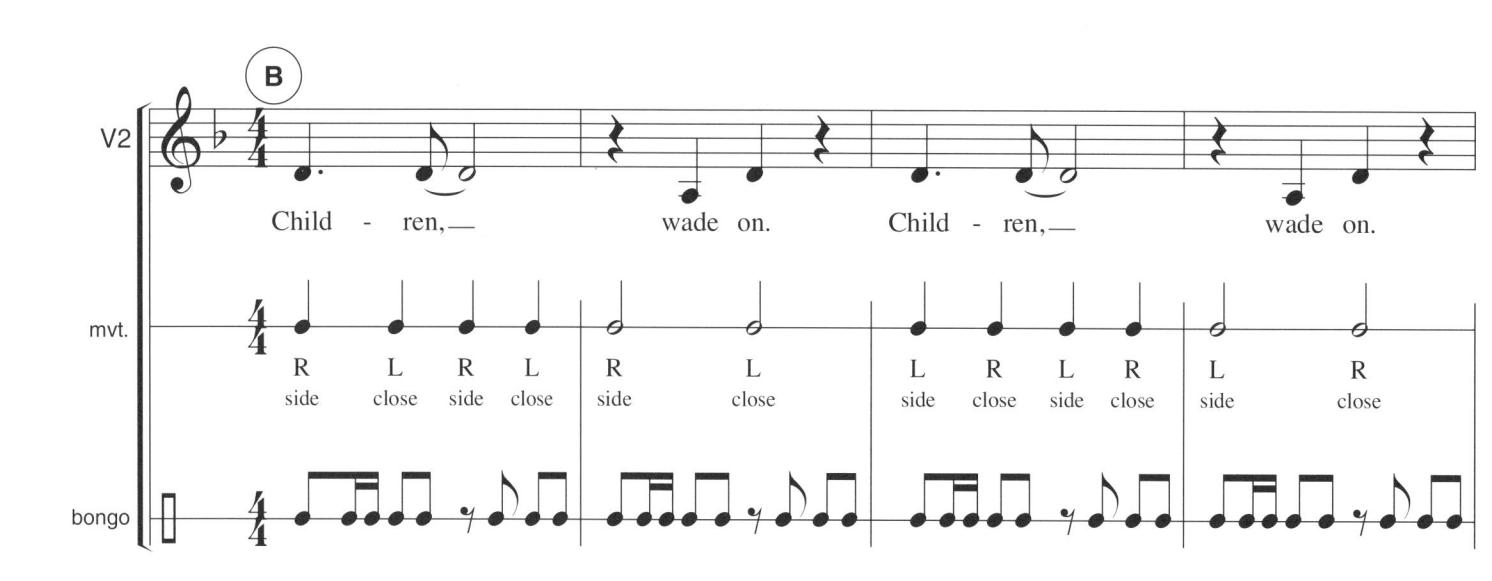

Spiritual
Arr. Dupont/Hiller

V2
Child - ren, wade on. Child - ren, wade on.
mvt.
R L R L R L L R L R L R
side close side close side close side close side close side close
bongo
C
V3
Oooh, Oooh,
Raise arms
Lower arms
mvt.
L R L R R L R L
fwd. touch bwd. touch
marac.
V3
Oooh, Oooh.
Raise arms
Lower arms
mvt.
L R L R R L R L
fwd. touch bwd. touch
marac.

Fire

Narrator: Passion, Creativity, Power, Drive!

All: Fire! (followed by a cluster chord on all barred instruments in C Pentatonic).

Narrator:
  Silent
  Embers smolder,
  Spread timidly; yet flames
  Deep within our souls awake with
  Courage.

Earth, Water, Fire
  Form: Additive
    (1) accompaniment, (2) V4, (3) V3, (4) V2.

Earth, Water, Fire

Presto — Dupont/Hiller

V2: Fire is burn-ing in-side, fire is burn-ing in-side us.
V3: Wa-ter slow-ly ris-ing. Wa-ter slow-ly ris-ing.
V4: Earth, turn-ing, spin-ning. Earth, turn-ing, 'round.
bongo
BX / BM / CBB

Tina Singu
  Form: Intro (Layer in the orchestration.)
    A Song with movement.
    B Speech ostinati layered in from bottom up.
    A Song with movement. All shout "Tina!" at the end.

Pronunciation and Translation:
  Tee-nah sing-goo leh-loo-voo-tae-o.   *Wat-shaw, wat-shaw, wat-shaw.*
  We are the burning fire.   We burn, we burn, we burn.

Tina Singu

African Folk Song
Arr. Dupont/Hiller

Ti - na Sing - u le - lu - vu - tae - o. Wat-sha, wat-sha, wat-sha.

Movement: Two lines of partners face each other. Section A has feet and hand movement; section B has only hand movement.

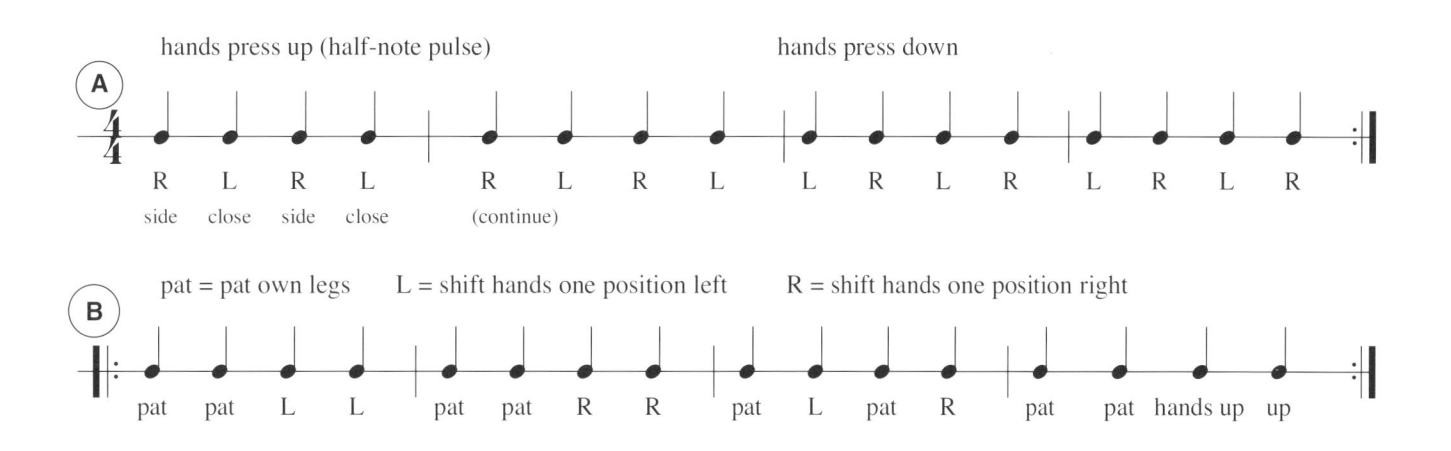

A hands press up (half-note pulse)   hands press down

R L R L R L R L L R L R L R L R
side close side close (continue)

B pat = pat own legs   L = shift hands one position left   R = shift hands one position right

pat pat L L pat pat R R pat L pat R pat pat hands up up

Fine

V1: Wat-sha, wat-sha, wat-sha, wat-sha, wat-sha. Ti - na!

V2: Wat-sha wat-sha, wat-sha, wat-sha wat-sha. Ti - na!

B — *D.C. al Fine*

V1: Rise! Gon-na' Rise! Gon-na' Rise! Gon-na' Rise! Gon-na'

V2: Wat-sha, wat-sha, wat-sha, Ti - na! Wat-sha, wat-sha, wat-sha, Ti - na!

V3: Burn! Burn! We are the burn-ing fire! Burn! Burn! We are the burn-ing fire!

Air

Narrator: Inspiration, Dreams, Wishes, Ideas!

All: Air! (followed by a cluster chord on all barred instruments in C Pentatonic).

Narrator:
Gentle
Breezes softly
Blow; whispering voices
Rise; life, breath, sorrow, joy and hope
Live on.

Earth, Water, Fire, Air
 Form: Additive
  (1) accompaniment, (2) V4, (3) V3, (4) V2, (5) V1.

Earth, Water, Fire, Air
Dupont/Hiller

Presto

V1: Air is flow-ing all a-round.

V2: Fire is burn-ing in-side, fire is burn-ing in-side us.

V3: Wa-ter slow-ly ris-ing. Wa-ter slow-ly ris-ing.

V4: Earth, turn-ing, spin-ning. Earth, turn-ing 'round.

bongo

BX / BM / CBB

Riding on the Wind
 Form: Intro: Two measures of accompaniment.
    Verse 1: All sing; movement group 1.
    Verse 2: All sing; movement group 2.
    Interlude: Movement groups stand in place.
    Verse 3: All sing; movement group 3.
    Coda

Riding on the Wind

Dupont/Hiller

Verse ♩ = 66

1. Soft and gen-tle breeze, whis-per through the trees, qui-ver gen-tle leaves, rid-ing on the wind.
3. Spir - it of the air, peace-ful with-out care, soft and si-lent prayer, rid-ing on the wind.

2. Soar a - bove the clouds, glid-ing strong and proud, migh-ty wings un-bound, rid-ing on the wind.

- 12 -

Movement: Students are divided into three movement groups, one for each verse. Everyone sings the entire song. Groups stand in place during the interlude and when other groups are moving.

The movement is poetic sign language, based on a combination of American Sign Language and Signed English, used for interpreting songs. Unless otherwise indicated, signs are performed with the right hand. Perform the sign for "riding on the wind" each time it occurs.

Group 1
- *Soft* — Palms upward, hands open and close gently
- *Breeze* — Hands indicate movement of wind, palms up
- *Whisper* — Hands vertical in front of chin, wiggle fingers
- *Tree* — Upright arm, representing a tree, supported by the horizontal left arm
- *Leaves* — Waving motion of right hand, lowered, as quivering leaves on a branch
- *Riding* — Gentle wavy movement of hand, representing floating

Group 2
- *Soar* — Raise both hands upwards with palms facing up
- *Clouds* — One hand over the other outlining the shape of clouds
- *Strong* — "S" hand shapes (both hands) pulled firmly away from chest
- *Proud* — Thumb of "A" hand shape points to self, moving up the chest
- *Mighty* — "S" hand shapes (both hands) pulled firmly away from chest
- *Wings* — Gently flap arms to indicate bird in flight

Group 3
- *Spirit* — Index finger and thumb spiral upward from palm of left hand
- *Peaceful* — Palms together, reverse position, then press downward
- *Without care* — Cross arms, middle fingers flick out and away from the shoulders
- *Soft* — Palms upward, hands open and close gently
- *Silent* — Index fingers in front of mouth; gently pull downward as hands open
- *Prayer* — Hands together clasped as if in prayer

All: Earth! Water! Fire! Air!

(Each word is followed by a cluster chord in C Pentatonic: Earth - BX/BM, Water - AX/AM, Fire - SX/SM, Air - AG/SG.)

Narrator:
Voices
Raise! Spirits dance!
Earth, Water, Fire, Air!
All that we are, all we will be;
Unite!

Round and Round (reprise)

Round and Round

Traditional
Arr. Dupont/Hiller

♩ = 130

BM — *trem.*

V / BM ost — Earth, wa - ter, fire and air.

1. V — Round and round the world is turn - ing.
2. Turn - ing al - ways

V / BM ost — Earth, wa - ter, fire and air. Earth, wa - ter,

3. V — 'round to morn - ing. And from morn - ing 'round to night.

V / BM ost — fire and air. Earth, wa - ter, fire and air.

- 14 -

Melody Appendix

You are permitted to copy any of the melodies and vocal harmonizations for the songs onto transparencies or printed copies to help students learn the songs.

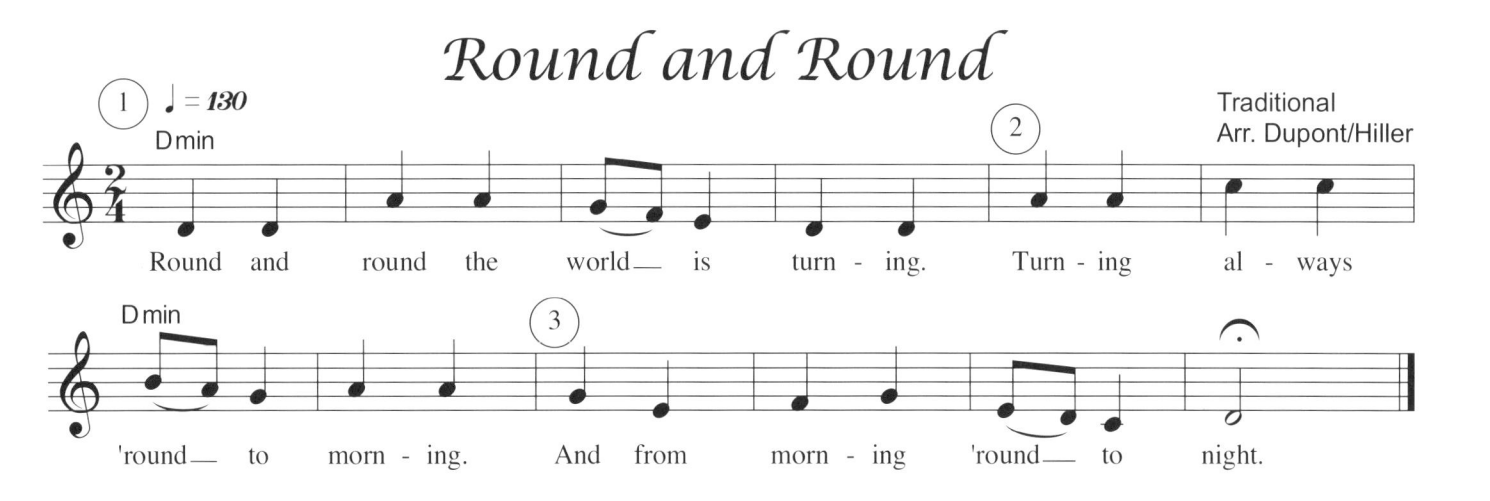

Round and Round

Traditional
Arr. Dupont/Hiller

Round and round the world is turn-ing. Turn-ing al-ways 'round to morn-ing. And from morn-ing 'round to night.

Earth Water, Fire, Air

Dupont/Hiller

V1: Air is flow-ing all a-round.

V2: Fire is burn-ing in-side, fire is burn-ing in-side us.

V3: Wa-ter slow-ly ris-ing. Wa-ter slow-ly ris-ing.

V4: Earth, turn-ing, spin-ning. Earth, turn-ing 'round.

La Tierra

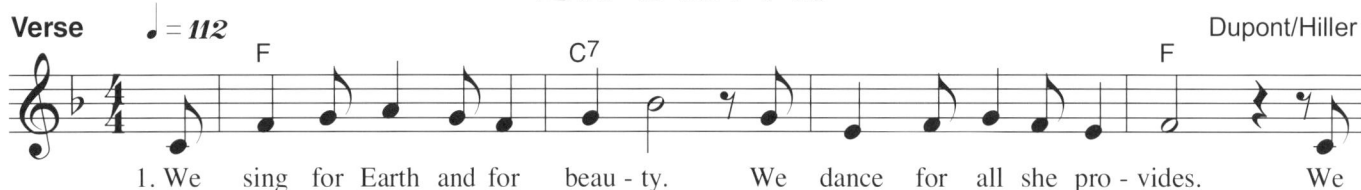

Dupont/Hiller

Verse ♩ = 112

1. We sing for Earth and for beau-ty. We dance for all she pro-vides. We lift our hearts and our voi-ces, and cel-e-brate side by side.
2. Oh, Moth-er Earth, we re-spect you. Your moun-tains, val-leys and shores. We stand as one to pro-tect you, and care for you ev-er-more.

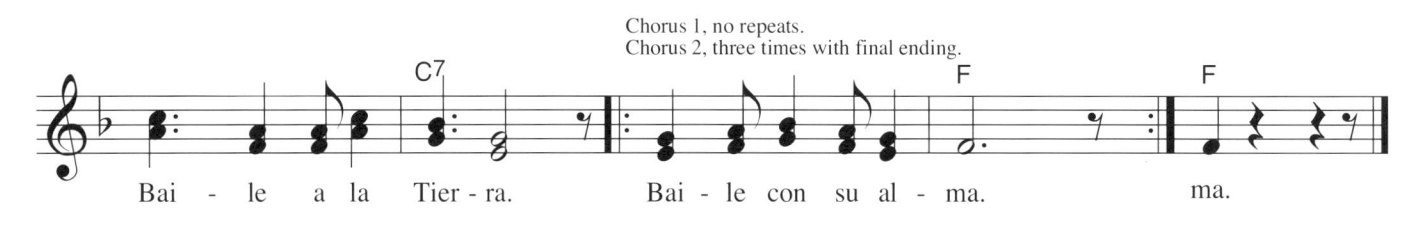

Chorus

Can - te a la Tier - ra. Can - te fuer - te y clar - o.

Chorus 1, no repeats.
Chorus 2, three times with final ending.

Bai - le a la Tier - ra. Bai - le con su al - ma. ma.

Wade in the Water

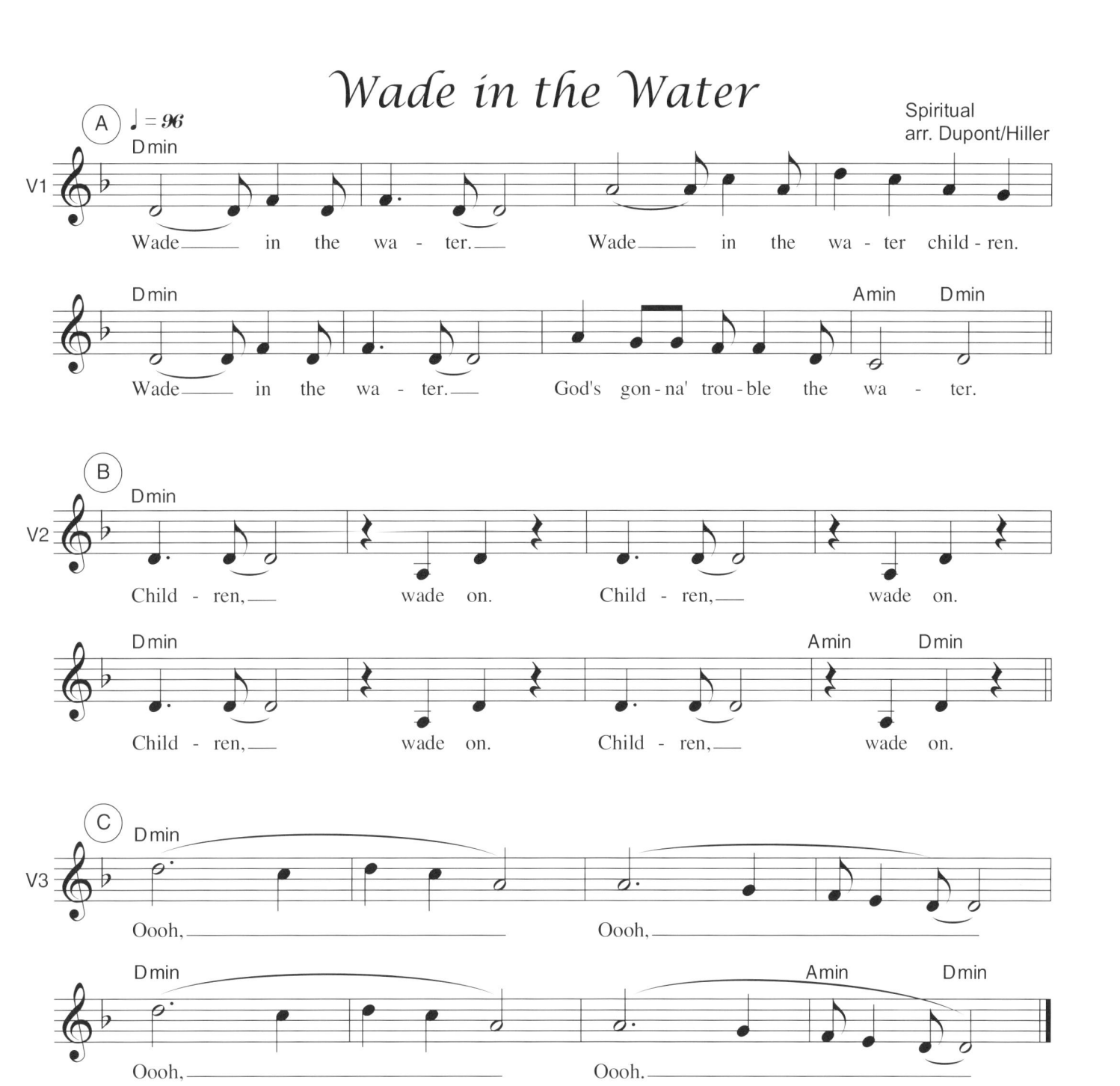

Spiritual
arr. Dupont/Hiller

A ♩ = 96

V1: Wade in the water. Wade in the water children.
Wade in the water. God's gon-na' trou-ble the wa-ter.

B

V2: Child-ren, wade on. Child-ren, wade on.
Child-ren, wade on. Child-ren, wade on.

C

V3: Oooh, Oooh,
Oooh, Oooh.

Tina Singu

African Folk Song
Arr. Dupont/Hiller

♩ = 132

A — All V:
Ti - na Sing - u le - lu - vu - tae - o. Wat-sha, wat-sha, wat-sha.

V1: Wat-sha, wat-sha, wat-sha, wat-sha, wat-sha. Ti - na!
V2: Wat-sha wat-sha, wat-sha, wat-sha wat-sha. Ti - na!

Fine

B — *D.C. al Fine*

V1: Rise! Gon-na' Rise! Gon-na' Rise! Gon-na' Rise! Gon-na'
V2: Wat-sha, wat-sha, wat-sha, Ti - na! Wat-sha, wat-sha, wat-sha, Ti - na!
V3: Burn! Burn! We are the burn-ing fire! Burn! Burn! We are the burn-ing fire!
V3 clap

Riding on the Wind

Dupont/Hiller

♩ = 66

Fine

E min — D — E min — D — E min

1. Soft and gen-tle breeze, whis-per through the trees, qui-ver gen-tle leaves, rid-ing on the wind.
3. Spir-it of the air, peace-ful with-out care, soft and si-lent prayer, rid-ing on the wind.

D.C. al Fine

E min — D — E min — D — E min

2. Soar a-bove the clouds, glid-ing strong and proud, migh-ty wings un-bound, rid-ing on the wind.

Fine Arts Connections

Art

Earth
Simultaneous Contrasts: Sun and Moon, by Robert Delaunay, 1913.
Spring Turning, by Grant Wood, 1936.
The Gleaners, by Jean-Francois Millet, 1857.

Water
Moonlight, Wood Island Light, by Winslow Homer, 1894.
Niagara, by Fredric Church, 1857.
Water Lilies, by Claude Monet, c. 1920.

Fire
Fire, by Sidney Goodman, 1979–1982.
The Burning of the Houses of Lords and Commons, by J.M.W. Turner, 1834.
Wall Explosion no. 1, by Roy Lichtenstein, 1964.

Air
A High Wind at Yeigiri, by Katsushika Hokusai, c.1830-35.
La Malediction (The Curse), by Rene Magritte, 1931.
The Queen of the Night, by Carl Friedrich Schinkel, 1815.

Music

Earth
Brandenburg Concertos, by J. S. Bach.
The Creation, by Franz Joseph Haydn.
Symphony No. 6 (Pastoral), by Ludwig van Beethoven.
Woodland Scenes, by Robert Schumann.

Water
Water Music Suite, by George Frederick Handel.
The Moldau, by Bedrich Smetana.
La Mer, by Claude Debussy.
On the Beautiful Blue Danube, by Johann Stauss II.

Fire
Rhapsody on a Theme of Paganini, by Sergei Rachmaninov.
March from Love of Three Oranges, by Sergei Prokofiev.
Two Rhapsodies for Violin and Orchestra, by Béla Bartók.

Air
Goldberg Variations, by J. S. Bach.
Suite in A Minor for Recorder and Strings, by Georg Telemann.
Concerto for Flute and Harp, by Wolfgang Amadeus Mozart.
Grand Canyon Suite, by Ferde Grofé.

Additional Orff-Schulwerk Publications

by

Don Dupont and Brian Hiller

✳

It's Elemental, Lessons that Engage, 2002.
Fifteen processed lessons for all elementary grades with
focus on rhythm, melody, texture, form and harmony.

It's Elemental, More Lessons that Engage, 2004.
Eighteen processed lessons for all elementary grades with
focus on rhythm, melody, texture, form, harmony and timbre.

Available from Memphis Musicraft Publications,
Music Stores and Catalogs.